I Can Help, Mommy

CHRISTIAN
SELF-DISCOVERY
SERIES

I Can Help, Mommy

By
Winifred Rouse Simpson

Illustrated by
Patricia Mattozzi

CONCORDIA®

Publishing House
St. Louis

Library of Congress Cataloging-in-Publication Data

Simpson, Winifred Rouse, 1937–
    I can help, Mommy

    (Self-concept book)
    Summary: Dede's willingness to help her mother around the house keeps the caring love of Jesus alive in her family.
    1. Helping behavior—Religious aspects—Christianity—Juvenile literature. 2. Children—Religious life. [1. Helpfulness. 2. Christian life] I. Mattozzi, Patricia, ill. II. Title. III. Series.

BV4571.2.S54   1986   248.8′2   86-990
ISBN 0-570-09112-8

---

1   2   3   4   5   6   7   8   9   10   KB   95   94   93   92   91   90   89   88   87   86

It was a bright, golden morning.
It was a glad-new day.

Dede opened her arms wide to the sunny day—
a special day all her own.

Jesus smiled at her from His picture.
Bright puddles of sunshine
splashed across the bedroom floor.

Dede's mother was singing outside the window
as she watered flowers in the garden . . .
and Dede wanted to help Mommy
in a very special, loving way.

Dede pulled the covers smooth on her bed
and fluffed the pillow . . . just so.

"See how I can help Mommy?" she said,
smiling at the picture of Jesus.

Dede washed her face,
then stood on her stool to hang up the towel.

"All by myself," she whispered.

In the kitchen
Dede found cereal and fruit
waiting for her on the table.

After eating,
Dede carried her dirty dishes to the sink
and put away the milk.

Laundry stood heaped before the washer.
Dede put all the white clothes together
in one big pile,
while Mommy sang in the garden.

The soft melody of Mommy's sweet song
about the caring love of Jesus
warmed Dede's heart
on this sunshiny, golden morning.

When Mommy went to the store,

Dede helped push the cart.

When they got home,
Mommy let Dede unpack the grocery sacks

and stack cans in the cupboard.

"My sweet girl is a BIG help today,"
said Mommy.
She smiled a loving smile

and took Dede in her arms.

"I wanted to help you, Mommy," said Dede.

"God wants us to help each other,"
said Mommy.
"Each thing you do for me
grows into a BIG help
in my busy, busy day!"

"And Jesus is helping, too!" said Dede.

Mommy's beautiful, loving smile
made a warm feeling
grow and grow inside Dede.

And Dede's warm feeling of helping love
grew on and on
all through that bright, golden day.

By love serve one another.
Galatians 5:13